# Word Spelling

## BOOK THREE

BY

## RONALD RIDOUT

ILLUSTRATED BY

## GEORGE W. ADAMSON, M.S.I.A.

# Ginn and Company Ltd

## BOOKS BY THE SAME AUTHOR

**Write in English,** Introductory Books 1 and 2 and Books 1-8: a new style of English Workbook providing a carefully graded course on understanding, using and writing English for all 6- to 12-year olds.

**Better English,** Introductory Book and Books 1-5: a complete English course from about 6-12 years; illustrated in colour.

**English Workbooks,** Introductory Books 1 and 2 and Books 1-8: a graded course in punctuation, spelling, vocabulary, comprehension and composition. The first two are intended for infants.

**English Workbooks for the Caribbean,** Books 1-8: a workbook course specially written for primary schools in the Caribbean; also suitable for immigrants; illustrated in colour.

**English Now,** Books 1-5: a complete course in magazine form for the less academic secondary pupil; illustrated in colour.

© RONALD RIDOUT 1957
Thirty-ninth impression 1993    059304
ISBN  0  602  20987  0

Published by Ginn and Company Ltd
Prebendal House, Parson's Fee, Aylesbury, Bucks HP20 2QZ

Printed in Great Britain by Henry Ling Ltd, Dorchester

# PREFACE

THE Introductory and eight main books of *Word Perfect Spelling* provide a systematic course in spelling and vocabulary for primary and secondary schools. Though in the first place it is correct spelling that they aim at, the books will at the same time help the pupil to gain complete mastery over the fundamental vocabulary needed by him at the various stages of his career.

Research has shown beyond dispute that the grouping of words in short lists according to common structural elements does facilitate their learning. The fact that words are held in the mind in certain patterns will, in both the short and the long run, enable them to be recalled more surely. In addition, it allows one key word to be used for unlocking many more. This, then, in the main, is the approach adopted, though other approaches have been used whenever they seemed to have a special contribution to make.

The course, however, does not end with the listing of words: it only begins there. The words have to be linked with the child's interests and brought to life by challenging activities. These activities are in themselves valuable aids to the teaching of English, but they have a vital function in improving spelling. They are based on the self-help principle whereby the pupil can hardly fail to get the right answer. This ensures that he will spell the word correctly when he writes it, and also use it correctly, so gaining the maximum benefit. For a child learns by doing, but he learns much more effectively by doing correctly.

In Book Three the first few pages are used to revise many of the patterns met in Book Two. Moreover, some of the later exercises also are used for revision, so that a sense of continuity is secured throughout the course. In all, some 560 words from earlier books are revised.

Although in Book Three the formation of correct habits is still the main foundation of learning to spell, an increasing attempt is made to explain the principles involved. As a consequence, simple rules are formulated on pages 8, 10, 18, 19, 25 and 29.

New patterns are introduced at a steady rate, and some 949 new words are met, many of which are practised more than once. It is considered more than ever important to ensure that the meaning of new words is thoroughly grasped, and in the exercises greater emphasis is now placed on this aspect of the work. A test for meaning is given at regular intervals on pages 13, 27 and 42.

For a more detailed discussion of the theory and practice of the course, the teacher is referred to the Teachers' Manual of *Word Perfect Spelling*. A set of diagnostic tests has been added to the Teachers' Manual, thus providing the teacher with a ready means of gauging the point at which any particular child or group should join the *Word Perfect Spelling* course.

HASLEMERE, 1976                                                    R.R.

brick

bless

bound

child

bust

block

club

damp

tie

grand

hook

why

belt

heel

card

while

| brick | bless | bound | child |
|-------|-------|-------|-------|
| bust | block | club | damp |
| tie | grand | hook | why |
| belt | heel | card | while |

1. Instead of br in brick write: tr, pr, th, st, cl, fl.
2. Instead of b in bust write: d, j, m, r, tr, cr.
3. Instead of t in tie write: l, p, d.
4. Instead of b in belt write: f, m, sm, sp.
5. Instead of bl in bless write: m, l, dr, pr, cr.
6. Instead of bl in block write: d, m, cl, fl, sh, fr, st, kn.
7. Instead of gr in grand write: b, h, l, s, st, husb, Engl, Scotl.
8. Instead of h in heel write: f, p, st, wh, kn.
9. Instead of b in bound write: f, h, m, p, r, s, w, gr, ar.
10. Instead of cl in club write: r, t, h, c, gr, sn, shr, scr.
11. Instead of h in hook write: b, c, l, r, t, sh, br, cr.
12. Instead of c in card write: y, h, l, cow, must, wiz, forw, cust.
13. Instead of ch in child write: m, w.
14. Instead of d in damp write: c, l, st, cr, tr, cl, sw.
15. Instead of wh in why write: m, fl, fr, cr, tr, dr, sh, sl.
16. Instead of wh in while write: f, m, p, t, st, sm, fert.
17. Instead of k in hook write: d, f, p, t, ter.
18. Instead of st in bust write: zz, mp, nch, ng, lb, cket.

| | | | |
|---|---|---|---|
| cake | leaf | frog | beach |
| spoon | twig | weed | spade |
| plate | branch | water | swimmer |
| bread | bird | tadpole | children |
| desk | dress | bacon | sheets |
| chalk | frock | soap | chair |
| pencils | skirt | eggs | brushes |
| teacher | gloves | butter | slippers |
| train | letters | eye | Tuesday |
| porter | words | ear | Wednesday |
| driver | paper | arm | Thursday |
| tickets | sentences | mouth | Friday |

These are words that you have met before. Can you still spell them? Write down the four most likely to be:

1. at the seaside
2. in a school
3. at the grocer's
4. on the tea-table
5. on a tree
6. in a pond

7. in a book
8. in a wardrobe
9. in a bedroom
10. on a calendar
11. at a station
12. belonging to a body

*23rd September, 93*

Once upon a time there was a young boy who was never tidy. He left his books on the chairs and his muddy shoes on the table. He put his fingers in the pudding and then wiped them on his shirt. He upset paint on his best clothes, and he dropped tooth-paste on the bathroom floor. He hardly ever brushed his hair. He was so untidy that we called him Tidy Tom as a joke.

*a soft mixture.*

*糊* *to clean with a cloth*

*muddy — wet earth*

| | | | |
|---|---|---|---|
| past | swing | wiped | muddy |
| paste | finger | tidy | dropped |
| fast | once | untidy | pudding |
| fasten | clothes | hardly | young |

*stick*

Write out ten words in the patch that can be built from the letters in this sentence:

OUR DONALD WAS FRYING THE POTATOES.

| slight | cool | done | sprang |
|--------|------|------|--------|
| fright | roof | none | sang |
| sight | broom | some | slang |
| might | stood | gone | rang |

| scrap | lift | again | died |
|-------|------|-------|------|
| strap | swift | against | cried |
| slack | silk | obtain | dried |
| swank | thinner | grain | carried |
| shabby | trigger | faint | married |

Can you arrange the first list in alphabetical order? Fright comes before might, because f comes before m in the alphabet. But if two words begin with the same letter, you must look at the second letters. Thus sight comes before slight, because i comes before l. In alphabetical order the same list is: fright, might, sight, slight.

Now arrange the other lists in alphabetical order, and number them 1 to 7.

8. Arrange this list in alphabetical order:
   tried, flight, foolish, something, finish, strain

ABCDEFGHIJKLMNOPQRSTUVWXYZ

*30th September, 1993.*

## PAGE FIVE (5)

1. three, two, one
2. one, two, three
3. two, one, three
4. three, four, five
5. five, six, seven
6. four, five, six
7. six, seven, eight
8. eight, seven, six
9. seven, eight, nine
10. nine, ten, eleven
11. seven, nine, eleven
12. eight, ten, twelve
13. thirteen, eleven, nine
14. fourteen, ten, six
15. five, ten, fifteen
16. four, sixteen, eight
17. seven, seventeen, eleven
18. seventeen, eighteen, nineteen
19. eighteen, nineteen, twenty

20. two, ten, twenty
21. one, ten, twenty-one
22. twenty-two, two, eleven
28. twenty, twenty-eight, two
30. ten, twenty, thirty
40. forty, thirty, twenty
50. forty, fifty, sixty
60. sixty, forty, twenty
70. thirty, fifty, seventy
80. sixty, seventy, eighty
90. ninety, one hundred, eighty
100. eighty, one hundred, ninety
106. ten, six, one hundred and six
346. three hundred and forty-six, one
1000. one thousand, two thousand

(a) Write down the figures and choose the right words to put after them. Begin like this: 1. one  2. two
(b) Write in words all the even numbers (2, 4, 6, 8, etc.) up to twenty.
(c) Write in words all the odd numbers (1, 3, 5, 7, etc.) up to nineteen.

| player | smoker | writer | gardener |
|--------|--------|--------|----------|
| owner | grocer | skater | footballer |
| farmer | driver | draper | hairdresser |
| butcher | miner | knitter | fishmonger |

In each sentence put in the right word from the patch.

1. A man who digs coal is called a *miner*.
2. A man who sells fish is called a *fishmonger*.
3. A *footballer* is someone who plays football.
4. A *butcher* is a man who sells meat.
5. The *hairdresser* — cut my hair yesterday.
6. The *owner* — of a cat is the person to whom it belongs.
7. The *writer* — of this letter is the person who sent it to me.
8. A person who runs a farm is called a *farmer* —.
9. Anyone who works in a garden is called a *worker*.
10. Anyone who takes part in a game is called a *player*.
11. The man who drives the bus is called the *driver*.
12. A *knitter* — is someone who knits.
13. The *draper* — sold me a pair of sheets and a towel.
14. A man who smokes cigarettes is called a *smoker*.
15. The *grocer* — sold me some bacon, eggs and cheese.
16. The *skater* — glided swiftly across the ice.

Betty bought a bit of butter,
But said, ' My bit of butter's bitter.
If I put it in my batter
It will make my batter bitter.
Better buy some fresher butter.'
Betty's mother said she'd let her,
So she bought some better butter
And it made her batter better.

batter

| better | buy | say | stop |
|--------|--------|--------|----------|
| bitter | bought | said | stopped |
| butter | ought | paid | stopping |
| batter | thought | afraid | stopper |

Stopper comes from the shorter word stop.
Write the shorter words that these come from:

1. rubber    *rub*    3. shopper    *shop*    5. planning    *plan*    7. bragging    *brag*
2. clapped    *clap*    4. runner    *run*    6. skater    *skat*    8. writing    *write*

Complete these tables:

| | | | | | | |
|---|---|---|---|---|---|---|
| 9. thin | thinner | thinnest | 15. flap | flapping | flapped |
| 10. slim | *slimmer* | slimmest | 16. drag | dragging | *dragged* |
| 11. *big* | *bigger* | biggest | 17. *fit* | fitting | *fitted* |
| 12. *hot* | hotter | *hottest* | 18. slip | *slipping* | *slipped* |
| 13. *worse* | worse | worst | 19. bring | *bringing* | brought |
| 14. good | *better* | best | 20. *say* | saying | *eased* |

# PAGE EIGHT (8)

| | | | |
|---|---|---|---|
| bus | buses | match | matches |
| dress | dresses | patch | patches |
| box | boxes | watch | watches |
| ditch | ditches | glove | gloves |
| brush | brushes | stove | stoves |
| branch | branches | month | months |

A singular noun means one only. A plural noun means more than one. To make a singular noun plural, we usually add just –s. But if the noun ends in a hissing letter like s, ch, sh or x, we have to add –es.

1. Write out the three plural nouns from the patch that have had just –s added to them.
2. Write out the nine plural nouns that have had –es added to them.

Write down the singular nouns from which each of these has been made:

3. branches  5. months  7. brushes  9. dishes
4. watches  6. gloves  8. glasses  10. churches

Write down the plural of these nouns:

11. match  13. bus  15. class  17. stove
12. patch  14. box  16. thrush  18 peach

*Plural numbers*

| | | |
|---|---|---|
| first | toffees *sweets* | |
| second | sugar | |
| third | coal | |
| fourth | carrots | |
| fifth | apples | |
| sixth | bottles | |
| seventh | chocolates | |
| eighth | potatoes | |

first
second
third
fourth
fifth
sixth
seventh
eighth

*Choc* *The*

GAR

Draw the bags and write on each to say what is inside.
Then write eight sentences, beginning like this:

1. The first bag is full of chocolates.
2. The second bag is full of . . .

Complete these:

9. one shoe but two shoes
10. one *dress* but two dresses
11. one *bus* but two buses
12. one fox but two *foxes*
13. one apple but six *apples*
14. one *match* but four matches

15. one chocolate but six *chocolates*
16. one *bottle* but two bottles
17. one church but two *churches*
18. one bush but nine *bushes*
19. one *dove* but two doves
20. one catch but eight *catches*

## PAGE TEN (10)

| | | | |
|---|---|---|---|
| aunt | ounce | instant | prince |
| uncle | inch | infant | princess |
| prison | bench | order | poem |
| apron | branch | border | poet |

The five vowels are: a, e, i, o, u. All the other letters of the alphabet are consonants.

We use a before a word that begins with a consonant, but we must use an before a word beginning with a vowel. Thus we say a lesson, but an inch. We say an odd uncle, but a broken branch.

1. Write out all the consonants.

2–17. Write out the words from the patch, putting a or an in front of each. Number them 2–17.

Write out these, putting a or an in each gap:

18. an ounce of pepper
19. in an instant
20. a long lesson
21. a rich prince
22. an empty bench
23. a short poem
24. an even border
25. an old scarf

26. a prince and a princess
27. an aunt in an apron
28. an oven in the kitchen
29. in a few minutes
30. an oil-can in his hand
31. as a gift
32. an apple a day
33. an oak tree and an elm

## PAGE ELEVEN (11)

Diana Brown likes drawing.
In the summer she sits on
the lawn and draws. One day
she drew a man going to work.
Then she drew the man falling
into the river. Next, she drew
another man diving into the

river after him. Last of all, she drew a large crowd.
Everyone was clapping the diver because he had saved
the other man from (drowning)

| town | word | law | crowd |
|------|------|------|-------|
| brown | worm | claw | worth |
| crown | work | straw | drawing |
| drown | world | lawn | worker |

1. Instead of s in <u>saw</u> write: l, p, r, j, cl, dr, str, outl.
2. Instead of d in <u>word</u> write: m, k, th, ld, se, st, ship.
3. Instead of l in <u>lawn</u> write: d, s, y, dr, sp.
4. Instead of t in <u>town</u> write: d, br, cr, cl, dr, fr, gr.

25th November

PAGE TWELVE (12)

| soft | shave | steam | shape |
|------|-------|-------|-------|
| often | slave | dream | cheat |
| soften | shade | scream | squeak |
| softly | grape | steal | after |

1. From the box below choose the six words that have the same short o vowel sound as you can hear in soft.

| both | soften | toffees | bottle | Joyce | lower |
|------|--------|---------|--------|-------|-------|
| often | loaf | shoes | pound | John | lorries |

2. From this box choose the six words that have the same long a vowel sound as you can hear in shape.

| grape | steam | shade | waste | fatter | April |
|-------|-------|-------|-------|--------|-------|
| cheat | shave | scream | fasten | draper | March |

Arrange these lists in alphabetical order. If in doubt, turn back to page 4.

| 3. Jane | 4. Richard | 5. Jean | 6. Charles |
|---------|-----------|---------|-----------|
| Grace | Betty | John | Andrew |
| Kate | Ronald | Jill | Thomas |
| George | Simon | James | Clare |
| David | Jessica | Judy | Cecil |

25th November 93

1. p a s t e / You can stick paper with this. (page 3)
2. e i g h t ✓ The number that comes after seven. (5)
3. b r a n c h e s / The plural of branch. (8)
4. s o f t e n / To make soft. (12)
5. o f t e n / Many times. (12)
6. w o r k e r / Anyone who works is called this. (11)
7. s u g a r / This is used to make food sweet. (9)
8. i n c h / There are twelve of these in a foot. (10)
9. y o u n g / The opposite of old. (3)
10. t w e n t y t w o / Twice eleven make this number. (5)
11. cheat
    s t e a l x To do something unfairly. (12)
12. b u t c h e r / A man who sells meat. (6)
13. f o o t b a l l e r / A person who plays football. (6)
14. o b t a i n / To get. (4)
15. broom
    s t o o d x A kind of brush. (4)
16. t a d p o l e / A baby frog. (2)
17. b u t t e r / Fat to spread on bread. (7)
18. d i t c h e s / The plural of ditch. (8)
19. f i s h m o n g e r / A man who sells fish. (6)
20. g r a p e / Wine is made from this fruit. (12)
21. d r e s s / The singular of dresses. (8)
22. W e d n e s d a y / The day after Tuesday. (2)
23. i n f a n t / A child under the age of seven. (10)

Let's make sure.

**(1)**

| lead | harm | water | joke |
|------|------|-------|------|
| beads | march | bathe | spoke |
| beach | part | seaside | close |
| teacher | party | diver | wrote |

**(2)**

| lift | dead | getting | band |
|------|------|---------|------|
| swift | bread | batting | blank |
| mist | ahead | better | crab |
| print | instead | flattest | slack |

**(3)**

| eight | sugar | prison | father |
|-------|-------|--------|--------|
| twelve | chocolates | lesson | brother |
| eighty | grocer | apron | baby |
| hundred | butcher | lemon | infant |

Mrs Brown walked down the road to do her shopping. She bought some bread from the baker and some meat from the butcher. Then she stepped across the street to the toyshop. There she bought a beach ball for Diana and a little spade for the baby.

*16th December.*

| January | May | September |
|---------|-----|-----------|
| February | June | October |
| March | July | November |
| April | August | December |

1. Write the month in which Christmas comes.
2. Write the month that it is now.
3. Write the month that it was last month.
4. Bonfire Night is on the fifth day of which month?
5. Suppose the year went backwards. Write the months in the order they would then come.
6. Write the month in which your birthday comes.
7. Write the months in alphabetical order. (March comes before May, and July comes before June.)

Write these sentences, putting in the right months:
8. The first month of the year is *January*.
9. *Dec* is the last month of the year.
10. After February comes *Mar*.
11. *Aug* comes after July.
12. *Feb* comes between January and March.
13. The months between July and October are *Aug* and *Nove*
14. —, — and — come between February and June.
15. —, —, — and — all end in –er.

Michael Short is just ten years old. He likes helping in the garden. His father has put him in charge of one of the flower-beds. There are forty sunflowers in this bed. They are very large and tall. They tower right up above Michael. There has not been a shower for a long time. So today Michael is busy watering his flowers.

*kind*

| sort | large | power | report |
|------|-------|-------|--------|
| sport | barge | flower | shower |
| short | charge | tower | busy |
| forty | great | towel | sunflower |

1. Instead of s in <u>sort</u> write: f, p, sh, rep, imp, exp, comf, transp.
2. Instead of er in <u>tower</u> write: el, n, ered.
3. Write the first list in alphabetical order.
4. Write the words from the patch that are the opposites of these: tiny, tall, idle, work, retreat.
5. Write these words in alphabetical order:
   shower   sunflower   port   power   sport   skirt

*4 large, short, busy, sport.*

*5 sunflower,*

| | | | |
|---|---|---|---|
| cheese | dozen | bottle | currants |
| kilo | packet | lemonade | sandwiches |
| gram | oranges | pepper | chocolates |
| bread | loaf | biscuit | potatoes |

2 a packet of biscuits

4 a bottle of lemonade

1 a packet of sandwiches

5 a loaf of bread

3 a kilo of cheese

6 100 grams of sweets

9 a dozen oranges

10 a box of chocolates

7 a sack of potatoes

8 $\frac{1}{2}$ kilo of currants

11 $\frac{1}{2}$ kilo of butter

12 25 grams of pepper

Draw the pictures and put the right description under each one.

| | | | |
|---|---|---|---|
| stick | sticking | tug | tugging |
| creep | creeping | drag | dragging |
| crawl | crawling | skid | skidding |
| | | chop | chopping |
| write | writing | knit | knitting |
| choose | choosing | stir | stirring |
| dance | dancing | strip | stripping |

Here are the rules about adding –ing:

(*a*) To most words you can just add –ing.

(*b*) But to words ending in e you must drop the e and then add –ing.   (Except words like see, be, tie.)

(*c*) To words that end with a single consonant before which comes a single vowel you must double the consonant and then add –ing.

From what word has each of these been formed?

| | | | |
|---|---|---|---|
| 1. dancing | 3. knitting | 5. stopping | 7. smoking |
| 2. crawling | 4. racing | 6. writing | 8. swimming |

9. Which rule do these follow?   Make three equal groups and mark them (*a*), (*b*), (*c*).

| | | |
|---|---|---|
| stare – staring | pray – praying | please – pleasing |
| bring – bringing | shop – shopping | knot – knotting |
| shine – shining | fetch – fetching | whir – whirring |

## PAGE NINETEEN (19)

| | | | |
|---|---|---|---|
| daisy | cities | empty | married |
| daisies | lilies | emptied | hurries |
| worry | cherries | carry | pities |
| worries | parties | carries | tidied |

To make the plural of a noun that ends in y and has a consonant before the y, you must change the y into i and then add –es. Thus we have: army—armies, story—stories.

Write the singular of the following nouns:
1. daisies  3. armies  5. lilies  7. stories  9. ladies
2. worries  4. cherries  6. parties  8. berries  10. babies

Write the plural of these nouns:
11. lily  13. story  15. fairy  17. spy  19. worry
12. party  14. army  16. copy  18. sky  20. baby

In the same way, if a verb ends in y with a consonant before the y, you must change the y into i before adding –es or –ed. Thus we have:

hurry—hurries—hurried,  reply—replies—replied

Add –es and –ed to these verbs. Begin like this:
21. bury—buries—buried

21. bury  23. carry  25. try  27. reply  29. marry
22. tidy  24. hurry  26. dry  28. pity  30. empty

| | | | |
|---|---|---|---|
| chief | happy | humble | cloth |
| thief | happen | grumble | clothes |
| field | rattle | simple | bath |
| piece | kettle | marble | bathe |

Write a word from the list that rhymes with:

1. battle   2. brief   3. shield   4. pimple   5. niece

*rattle   thrief   field   simple   piece*

Write from the patch the word meaning the opposite of:

6. unhappy   7. proud   8. difficult   9. whole

*happy   humble   simple   Piece*

10. Write out the six words that end in –le.

Grumbling is made from the shorter word grumble. Write the shorter words that these are made from:

11. tumbling  12. rattling  13. grumbled  14. rumbling

*tumble   rattle   grumble   rumble*

15. Write the eight words from the patch that can be built from these letters: A B C D E F H I L M P R S T U.

Arrange each list below in alphabetical order:

| 16. Ruth | 17. Robert | 18. cattle | 19. Jones |
|---|---|---|---|
| Tony | Albert | battle | Thomas |
| Roger | Arthur | belief | Taylor |
| Mary | Henry | chief | Jennings |
| Molly | Harry | field | Price |

*3rd February, 94.*

I – N spells in.
I was in my kitchen
Doing a little stitching.
Old Father Nimble
Came and took my thimble.
I fetched a great big stone
And knocked him on the funny bone.
O – U – T spells out.

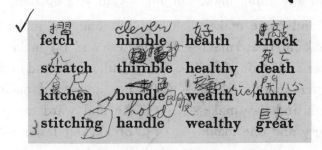

| | | | |
|---|---|---|---|
| fetch | nimble | health | knock |
| scratch | thimble | healthy | death |
| kitchen | bundle | wealth | funny |
| stitching | handle | wealthy | great |

Write the words from the patch that rhyme with:
1. candle  2. shock  3. sunny  4. thimble  5. catch

6. Instead of f in <u>fetch</u> write: str, sk. *stretch  sketch*
7. Instead of st in <u>stitch</u> write: w, d, p, sw, tw. *witch*
8. Instead of scr in <u>scratch</u> write: c, m, p, sn, th. *caratch*
9. Instead of b in <u>bone</u> write: st, ph, al, thr. *stone*
10. Instead of th in <u>death</u> write: d, f, lt, dly. *dea*
11. Instead of tch in <u>fetch</u> write: ll, lt, nce, nder, rry.

Make new words by adding y to these:
12. dust  14. wealth  16. luck  18. cloud
13. rust  15. health  17. pluck  19. frost

| | | | |
|---|---|---|---|
| someone | anyone | nowhere | towards |
| something | anything | nothing | (afterwards) |
| sometimes | anybody | nobody | forward |
| somewhere | anywhere | everywhere | (together) |

<u>No</u> and <u>thing</u> make <u>nothing</u>.   Can you do these?

1. Be and come make *become.*
2. Black and board make *blackboard.*
3. After and noon make *afternoon.*
4. Butter and fly make *Butterfly.*
5. Birth and day make *Birthday.*
6. Every and one make *Everyone.*
7. How and ever make *however.*
8. Rain and bow make *Rainbow.*
9. But and ton make *button.*
10. Less and on make *lesson.*
11. Under and stand make *under.*
12. For and ward make *forward.*
13. Re and ward make *Reward.*
14. Break and fast make *Breakfast.*
15. Be and fore make *Before.*
16. Be and lieve make *Believe.*

Pair each word with its opposite.   Begin like this:

17. something—nothing
18. nowhere

| | | | |
|---|---|---|---|
| 17. something | poor | 23. afterwards | nobody |
| 18. nowhere | heavy | 24. black | saving |
| 19. light | nothing | 25. great | before |
| 20. hating | backward | 26. spending | white |
| 21. wealthy | loving | 27. often | little |
| 22. forward | somewhere | 28. somebody | never |

This is the key of a country.
In that country there is a county.
In that county there is a village.
In that village there is a square.
In that square there is a cottage.
In that cottage there is a room.
In that room there is a table.
On that table there is a basket,
    And in that basket there are some flowers.

| village | town | county | table |
|---------|------|--------|-------|
| cottage | flower | country | unable |
| cabbage | dare | mountain | basket |
| garage | square | fountain | ticket |

1. Write the jingle backwards, beginning like this :
    The flowers were in the basket.
    The basket was on
2. Instead of d in <u>d</u>are write : c, f, r, sp, st, sq, sh, sc, aw, bew.
3. Instead of t in <u>t</u>icket write : w, cr.
4. Instead of t in <u>t</u>able write : st. c, f, un, cap.
5 Instead of fl in <u>fl</u>ower write : p, t, sh.

   Write the plural of these nouns :
6. county  7. country  8. ferry  9. square  10. basket

*pains*
| aches | our | never | soon |
|-------|-----|-------|------|
*a big monken* *ball*
| ape | sour | every | steer |
*round* *allow*
| shape | aloud | shed | idea |
*hard*
| busy | enough | roar | area |
*angry*

Draw your own puzzle
Then use some of the
words from the patch to
solve it. Here are the
clues :

**Across**

1. To guide.
3. Pains that go on and on.
5. Belonging to us.
7. Tail-less animal that can walk on two feet.
8. The opposite of always.
9. Not in a whisper.

**Down**

1. In a short time.
2. A loud deep sound.
3. Amount of surface.
4. A building used to store things.
6. The opposite of down.

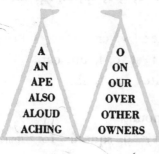

```
A          O
AN         ON
APE        OUR
ALSO       OVER
ALOUD      OTHER
ACHING     OWNERS
```

These are word tents. Each
word has to have one more
letter than the one above it.
Make another tent, begin-
ning with A. Then make
one with the words begin-
ning with I.

If you want to keep healthy
you must make sure
that your teeth are clean.
It is a good plan
to brush them every night
before going to bed.
In the picture you can see
John in the bathroom.
He has a tube of tooth-paste.
He is just going to put some
on his tooth-brush.
What kind of tooth-paste
do you use for your teeth?

| tub | tube | rude | pure |
|-----|------|------|------|
| cub | cube | tune | sure |
| cur | cure | fuse | picture |
| us | use | refuse | excuse |

Notice that when you add a silent e to tub, the short vowel sound u becomes a long vowel sound. Make new words by adding a silent e to:

1. slid  2. cub  3. slop  4. spin  5. cur  6. scrap.

Curing comes from cure. What do these come from?
7. using  8. refusing  9. sliding  10. excusing  11. tuning

| high | knee | lamb | quite |
| light | kneel | comb | alone |
| brought | knock | climb | above |
| thought | knot | thumb | starve |

Notice the silent letters. In the first list gh is silent. In the second it is k. In the third it is b, and in the last it is e.

Arrange these words in four lists in the same way:

| knit | strike | climbing | nought |
| thought | scrape | knitting | thumbs |
| axe | knelt | kneeling | brought |
| crumb | fought | combing | flame |

Pair each numbered word with its opposite.

| 1. high | many | 9. bought | wrong |
| 2. above | dull | 10. right | rude |
| 3. few | empty | 11. light | ill |
| 4. bright | hard | 12. alive | sold |
| 5. full | low | 13. liked | highest |
| 6. asleep | below | 14. lowest | dead |
| 7. easy | took away | 15. polite | hated |
| 8. brought | awake | 16. healthy | heavy |

1. [ ][ ][a][g][e] Place to keep a car. (page 23)

2. [ ][ ][i][e][s] Plural of daisy. (19)

3. [ ][e][e][ ] To go down on your knees. (26)

4. [ ][ ][t][y] To take everything out. (19)

5. [ ][ ][ ][ ] The opposite of polite. (25)

6. [ ][ ][t][h][ ] Means the same as rich. (21)

7. [ ][c][h][ ] Pains that go on and on. (24)

8. [ ][ ][ ][ ][y] The first month of the year. (15)

9. [ ][o][w][ ] You can dry your hands on this. (16)

10. [ ][ ][y] You are this when you have a lot to do. (16)

11. [ ][ ][e][a] This comes from boiling water. (12)

12. [ ][t][ ] To go and get. (21)

13. [ ][ ][ ] You can make dresses from this material. (20)

14. [ ][ ][ ][ ][ ] The plural of orange. (17)

15. [ ][ ][ ][ ] To pick out. (18)

16. [ ][ ][ ][ ] The singular of worries. (19)

17. [ ][ ][ ][ ][ ] A person who knits. (6)

18. [ ][ ][ ][ ] Means the same as a part. (20)

19. [ ][ ][ ][ ] You take hold of this. (21)

20. [ ][ ][ ][ ] You carry your shopping in this. (23)

21. [ ][ ][ ][ ][ ] The opposite of everything. (22)

22. [ ][ ][ ][ ] To have nothing to eat. (26)

23. [ ][ ][ ][ ] This is a person who steals. (20)

Let's make sure.

(4)

| chew | price | began | float |
|------|-------|-------|-------|
| flew | twice | begun | coast |
| crew | clay | being | soak |
| threw | pray | become | roar |

(5)

| soil | vain | better | rage |
|------|------|--------|------|
| spoil | rail | cutter | trade |
| coin | laid | knitter | grave |
| voice | raise | spanner | waste |

(6)

| bread | enter | dance | work |
|-------|-------|-------|------|
| spread | tender | dancing | since |
| instead | spider | chance | change |
| ready | poker | glance | changing |

Jane likes helping her mother. She always lays the table for tea. Afterwards she washes up and dries the dishes. On Saturday mornings she polishes the floor, and then goes shopping.

| half | halves | wife | wives |
|------|--------|------|-------|
| shelf | shelves | knife | knives |
| loaf | loaves | thief | thieves |
| leaf | leaves | himself | themselves |

When a noun ends in f, you often have to change the f into v and then add –es to make the plural.

With a word ending in –fe, you must change the f into v and add only –s, because the e is already there.

Write the singular of these nouns:

1. leaves    3. halves    5. thieves    7. wolves
2. wives     4. calves    6. scarves    8. lives

Write the plural of these nouns:

9. shelf   11. calf    13. knife   15. life    17. himself
10. thief  12. wife    14. wolf    16. elf     18. scarf

Arrange each list in alphabetical order:

| 19. shelves | 20. elves | 21. knots | 22. excuses |
|-------------|-----------|-----------|-------------|
| loaves | flowers | sights | cubes |
| thieves | thumbs | keys | combs |
| leaves | knees | thrushes | tubes |
| wives | calves | teeth | themselves |
| halves | crumbs | stitches | towers |
| knives | churches | showers | chocolates |

On Easter Monday John had breakfast early, so that he could visit the zoo. It was not a long journey, and he was soon there. He paid his money and went inside. He looked at the lions, tigers and bears first. Then he visited the cages where the monkeys lived. There he met a friend. No, it was not a monkey! It was Peter from the next street. After they had seen all the monkeys, they had a ride together on an elephant.

| lion | wolf | money | Easter |
| tiger | deer | monkey | early |
| bear | camel | journey | friend |
| zebra | visit | elephant | breakfast |

Write the singular of:

1. camels   3. wolves   5. monkeys   7. tigers
2. friends   4. journeys   6. calves   8. watches

Make new words by adding these endings to visit:

9. –s   10. –ed   11. –ing   12. –or   13. –ors

Write the words from the patch that rhyme with:

14. honey   15. steer   16. rare   17. yearly   18. mend

| | | | |
|---|---|---|---|
| bus | aeroplane | bicycle | liner |
| car | seaplane | tricycle | yacht |
| lorry | helicopter | motor-cycle | lifeboat |
| tractor | airliner | scooter | submarine |

Write these, putting in the words from the patch:

1. A — has pedals and two wheels.
2. A — has pedals and three wheels.
3. A — is a bicycle driven by a motor.
4. A child drives a — by pushing on the ground with one foot. It is also a name for a light motor-cycle.
5. A large passenger boat is called a —.
6. Goods are taken by road in a —.
7. A — is like a big car that carries many people.
8. Four or five people can travel by road in a —.
9. An — is driven by propellers or jets and can land only on the ground.
10. A —, however, can land on water.
11. A — can land almost straight down.
12. A sailing boat used for racing is called a —.
13. An — is an aeroplane that carries many passengers.
14. A — is used for pulling things over rough ground.
15. A ship that sails under water is called a —.
16. A — is used for making rescues at sea.

| ragged | rascal | clever | pickled |
|--------|--------|--------|---------|
| rugged | stripe | river  | tickled |
| pepper | piper  | polite | paddled |
| rubber | wiper  | invite | cuddled |

Peter Piper picked a peck of pickled pepper;
A peck of pickled pepper Peter Piper picked.
If Peter Piper picked a peck of pickled pepper,
Where is the peck of pickled pepper Peter Piper picked?

Round and round the rugged rock
The ragged rascal ran.
Say how many R's in that
And you're a clever man.

| odd   | build    | listen  | buy    |
|-------|----------|---------|--------|
| usual | built    | earth   | laugh  |
| music | building | plenty  | people |
| huge  | sign     | present | view   |

This is an extra list. You will often need these odd words; so make sure you can spell them.

1. Write the eight words that can be built from the letters of this sentence:

   WAS ROBIN HOOD BOLD ENOUGH TO WIN?

2. Write in alphabetical order the eight that are left.

There was an old man who said, " Well!
Will nobody answer this bell?
I have pulled day and night
Till my hair has turned white,
But nobody answers the bell! "

| loose | wear | quick | answer |
| goose | bear | quickly | freeze |
| geese | tear | quiet | weary |
| cheese | pear | quietly | question |

Write the adjectives from which these adverbs come:

1. quickly   3. loosely   5. rudely   7. selfishly
2. quietly   4. politely   6. silently   8. wrongly

Choose one of the adverbs above to fill each gap:

9. John ran — and soon caught the goose.
10. Susan answered the question quite — when she said that two and two make five.
11. The picture was hanging so — that it fell down as soon as I touched it.
12. Christopher very — left no pudding for his sister.
13. With a soft voice you can speak — but never —.
14. The opposite of speaking — is speaking —.

| | | | |
|---|---|---|---|
| shirt | penny | won | month |
| skirt | pennies | wonder | monk |
| birth | pence | wonderful | squirt |
| third | fence | Monday | birthday |

| 1980 | JANUARY | | | | 1980 |
|---|---|---|---|---|---|
| Sunday | | 6 | 13 | 20 | 27 |
| Monday | | 7 | 14 | 21 | 28 |
| Tuesday | 1 | 8 | 15 | 22 | 29 |
| Wednesday | 2 | 9 | 16 | 23 | 30 |
| Thursday | 3 | 10 | 17 | 24 | 31 |
| Friday | 4 | 11 | 18 | 25 | |
| Saturday | 5 | 12 | 19 | 26 | |

1. Margaret : 2nd January
2. Philip : 5th January
3. Paul : 9th January
4. Diana : 12th January
5. Ian : 16th January
6. Elizabeth : 19th January
7. Sheila : 23rd January
8. Norman : 26th January
9. Alan : 31st January

On the right above are the dates of the birthdays of nine children. On what days will their birthdays be in 1980? Begin your answers like this : 1. *Margaret's birthday will be on a Wednesday.*

Arrange each of these lists in alphabetical order :

| 10. Christine | 11. Michael | 12. Elizabeth | 13. Morris |
|---|---|---|---|
| Jennifer | Margaret | Ernest | Austin |
| Colin | Douglas | Donald | Hillman |
| John | David | Derek | Standard |
| Judith | Arthur | Diana | Singer |
| Charles | Andrew | Ethel | Ford |

Here is the weather forecast. Today it will be warm and sunny in Wales and the south of England. In the north of England there will be some showers late in the day. In Scotland it will be foggy at first, and in the afternoon there may be thunder-storms. Tomorrow's outlook is less good. It  will be dull and cloudy over the whole of the British Isles, and rain is likely to spread from the west.

| yesterday | thunder | foggy | England |
|---|---|---|---|
| tomorrow | lightning | sunny | Scotland |
| weather | sunshine | storm | Wales |
| forecast | dull | gale | British Isles |

1. Instead of w in weather write: f, l, h.
2. In front of under write: th, bl, pl.
3. Instead of ll in dull write: st, sk, ck, sty, ster.
4. Instead of st in frost write: ck, g, m, nt, sty, wn.
5. Instead of Eng in England write: Scot, Ire, is, main, Hol.
6. Instead of m in storm write: e, k, my, y.
7. Instead of g in gale write: p, t, s, st, sc, wh.

| | | | |
|---|---|---|---|
| reply | hammer | sorry | mother |
| repeat | stammer | silly | copper |
| funny | summer | hilly | river |
| furry | sudden | spilling | penny |

Each of these words has two parts. Thus, summer is made up of sum and mer. We call these parts syllables. Summer has two syllables.

From each group of syllables below, make up the two words asked for. All the words are in the patch.

| ny  pen  fun |
|---|

1. a copper coin
2. another word for amusing

| er  riv  moth |
|---|

3. a woman who has children
4. a very large stream

| fur  sor  ry |
|---|

5. covered with fur
6. feeling regret

| peat  ply  re |
|---|

7. to say again
8. to give an answer

| mer  ham  sum |
|---|

9. tool for knocking in nails
10. the season that follows spring

| ly  hil  sil |
|---|

11. full of hills
12. not sensible

| polish | forgive | across | afraid |
|--------|---------|--------|--------|
| finish | forget | above | forest |
| punish | forbid | around | English |
| furnish | forward | alike | British |

Add the missing syllable to each of these, to make one of the words in the patch :

1. — give     5. pol —     9. — ward     13. fin —
2. — bove     6. Eng —     10. — round     14. — fraid
3. — est     7. Bri —     11. pun —     15. furn —
4. — get     8. — bid     12. — like     16. — cross

Divide these words into two syllables each :

17. cannot     21. upstairs     25. between     29. England
18. before     22. himself     26. carpet     30. Tuesday
19. forget     23. summer     27. unless     31. July
20. across     24. snowdrop     28. invite     32. Betty

Some words have three syllables. Thus, afternoon can be divided like this: af – ter – noon. (Notice that every syllable has a vowel in it.)

Divide these words into three syllables each:

33. yesterday     37. November     41. polishing
34. suddenly     38. December     42. punishment
35. understand     39. forgiven     43. forbidden
36. understood     40. forgotten     44. butterfly

| | | | |
|---|---|---|---|
| baked | tried | nibbled | viewed |
| enjoyed | stole | gobbled | inspected |
| munched | fought | captured | reached |
| wanted | lifted | quartered | heated |
| divided | upset | pointed | |
| opened | kept | jumped | |

Write out this alphabet, putting in the right words from the patch. The first three have been done to show you how to carry on.

A was an apple pie.　　I — it.　　　　P — at it.
B baked it.　　　　　J — for it.　　　Q — it.
C captured it.　　　　K — it.　　　　R — for it.
D — it.　　　　　　　L — it.　　　　S — it.
E — it.　　　　　　　M — it.　　　　T — it.
F — for it.　　　　　N — it.　　　　U — it.
G — it.　　　　　　　O — it.　　　　V — it.
H — it.　　　　　　　　　　　　　　W — it.

X Y Z all longed for it.

Andrew was a lucky boy. His parents took him for a holiday in France. They went to London Airport by coach. They saw many aeroplanes taking off and touching down. Soon Andrew was climbing into an airliner. The pilot revved up the engine. The airliner raced down the runway. A moment later they were airborne. Far below them they could see the river, roads and houses growing smaller and smaller.

| | | | |
|---|---|---|---|
| France | airport | revved | pilot |
| London | airliner | raced | engine |
| Andrew | airborne | touching | parents |
| aeroplane | coach | climbing | holiday |

| | | | |
|---|---|---|---|
| return | lose | excite | prove |
| remain | loser | exciting | improve |
| repair | move | enjoy | depart |
| remark | remove | enjoyable | suddenly |

The vowels have been left out. Put them in, and write out the words and their meanings.

1. R – M – V –        To take away.
2. R – M – – N        To stay where you are.
3. D – P – R T        To go away.
4. R – T – R N        To come back.
5. L – S – R          A person who loses.
6. S – D D – N L Y    All of a sudden.
7. – N J – Y – B L –  Able to be enjoyed.
8. – M P R – V –      To become better.
9. R – P – – R        To make good again.
10. – X C – T – N G   Which stirs up one's feelings.

Can you make these into words ending in –ing?

11. excite    14. enjoy    17. remove    20. begin
12. lose      15. repair   18. dig       21. waste
13. improve   16. invite   19. forget    22. glide

Make adjectives by adding –able to these verbs:
23. enjoy  24. remark  25. agree  26. obtain  27. suit

Make adverbs by adding –ly to these adjectives:
28. sudden  29. quiet  30. fair  31. unfair  32. clever

| thirst | dirty | hasty | tiny |
| thirsty | stormy | icy | nasty |
| taste | weary | tidy | noisy |
| tasty | sleepy | rosy | wavy |

Make new words by adding y to these:

| | | | |
|---|---|---|---|
| 1. rain | 4. thirst | 7. curl | 10. fair |
| 2. dirt | 5. health | 8. bus | 11. read |
| 3. wind | 6. wealth | 9. part | 12. ever |

Notice that when you add y to a word ending in a silent e, like taste, you have to drop the e and then add y. Now make new words by adding y to these:

| | | | |
|---|---|---|---|
| 13. haste | 16. shine | 19. bone | 22. laze |
| 14. ice | 17. shade | 20. stone | 23. craze |
| 15. wave | 18. rose | 21. noise | 24. juice |

Pair each adjective with its opposite.

| | | | | |
|---|---|---|---|---|
| 25. tasty | quiet | | 32. nasty | ugly |
| 26. noisy | full | | 33. ready | shaky |
| 27. dirty | tasteless | | 34. steady | nice |
| 28. empty | straight | | 35. tiny | polite |
| 29. cloudy | clean | | 36. early | huge |
| 30. heavy | light | | 37. pretty | late |
| 31. wavy | sunny | | 38. rude | unready |

1. ☐ ☐ c h ☐ ☐ Place where you cook. (page 21)
2. ☐ ☐ p h ☐ ☐ Largest animal in the world. (30)
3. ☐ ☐ e r A person who loses. (40)
4. ☐ o l ☐ ☐ ☐ The opposite of rude. (32)
5. ☐ ☐ ☐ ☐ ☐ o w The day after today (35)
6. ☐ z ☐ Another way of saying twelve. (17)
7. ☐ ☐ ☐ i e s The plural of penny. (34)
8. ☐ ☐ ☐ t y Needing a drink. (41)
9. ☐ o o ☐ The opposite of tight. (33)
10. ☐ ☐ ☐ v ☐ The plural of thief. (29)
11. ☐ ☐ m a ☐ ☐ A ship that sails under the water. (31)
12. ☐ w ☐ You give this to a question. (33)
13. ☐ ☐ ☐ ☐ The one before the fourth. (34)
14. ☐ ☐ ☐ ☐ Making a lot of noise. (41)
15. ☐ ☐ ☐ ☐ To come back. (40)
16. ☐ ☐ ☐ ☐ ☐ Mother and father. (39)
17. ☐ b b ☐ ☐ Took little bites. (38)
18. ☐ ☐ ☐ ☐ A large wood. (37)
19. ☐ ☐ ☐ ☐ The season that follows spring. (36)
20. ☐ ☐ ☐ Having plenty to do. (16)
21. ☐ ☐ ☐ d s The opposite of away from. (22)
22. ☐ ☐ ☐ ☐ ☐ ☐ ☐ ☐ A person who cuts hair. (6)
23. ☐ ☐ ☐ ☐ Means the same as to end. (37)

Let's make sure.

(7)

| path | utter | treat | gather |
|------|-------|-------|--------|
| bath | suffer | eaten | stream |
| rather | rubber | beaten | manner |
| father | offer | broken | matter |

(8)

| dinner | brought | wool | battle |
|--------|---------|------|--------|
| ladder | fought | stool | muddle |
| rabbit | worse | bloom | little |
| bottom | worst | blood | settle |

(9)

| charm | cheer | friend | cradle |
|-------|-------|--------|--------|
| charge | feeling | people | gentle |
| farmer | indeed | women | needle |
| army | weedy | children | tumble |

Last year we spent a whole month of our summer holidays in the country. We stayed on Uncle John's farm. I liked riding on the tractor best, but Judy thought that riding the pony was better.

## For extra work

(1)

| | | | |
|---|---|---|---|
| careless | heart | pillow | nurse |
| careful | hearth | yellow | purse |
| useful | heaven | shallow | burst |
| useless | dreadful | hollow | burnt |

(2)

| | | | |
|---|---|---|---|
| person | content | illness | scout |
| pardon | moment | darkness | guide |
| serve | defend | shadow | whistle |
| term | pretend | dying | explore |

(3)

| | | | |
|---|---|---|---|
| anger | cover | chimney | station |
| angry | silver | cupboard | travel |
| hunger | shelter | animal | voyage |
| hungry | murder | history | adventure |

(4)

| | | | |
|---|---|---|---|
| darling | beginning | easy | Christmas |
| starling | together | easier | Christine |
| partner | enough | heavy | Christopher |
| farther | cough | heavier | Christian |